In the Company of Angels

Robert Strand

Volume 3

Crossings Book Club
Garden City, New York

Contents

Dedication

This book is the result of many people who
are willing and trusting enough to share their
experiences with us. Without them there would
be no more collections of angel stories.
Thank you, thank you!

Introduction

There is a great desire today to know more about the unseen or spiritual world. In this unseen realm, which is such an integral part of God's universe, we are aware of powerful, exciting, and wonderful forces at work behind the scenes of our reality. People continue to be fascinated with angels, and the hunger for their stories has not yet been satisfied and may never be. Angels are beings who apparently move faster than the speed of light and can intervene in human affairs both large and small. These affairs may encompass nations or be as small as the concerns of a little child. Angels are involved in carrying out the will of their Master—God.

We have been discovering many unique ways in which these wonderful beings perform their ministry. They can stand guard, protect us, convey messages to us, help us, offer comfort when we need it, and even watch over what happens in the church where we worship and more! Most importantly they engage in cosmic, spiritual battles that we are not even aware are taking place.

Many people have been exposed to a lot of misinformation or bad information about angels. Too much of this has come from some poor resources. There's a lot of angel lore, ancient stories, myths, and, of course, experiences from people who claim to have had such encounters. Many writers and people who share such misinformation have gone down every avenue of exploration to make their discoveries known, except the only genuine, true source of absolute truth—the Bible, God's

Word! Everything you have heard or are reading about angels and their ministry must be measured against the standard of truth—God's Word.

When you go to the Bible for your research and insight into angels you will not be disappointed! The Bible is full of stories about them! More than half—thirty-four to be exact—of the Bible's sixty-six books mention angels and often in great detail. Every writer of the New Testament affirms the existence of angels. The words "angel" or "angels" can be found more than 260 times in the Bible. This is obviously not some minor, obscure subject that is hidden so only biblical scholars can unearth it.

Maybe the most important fact is that Jesus Christ talked about angels as being real and involved in many phases of human activity. He even stated He could have called legions of them to come to His rescue. So we are not talking or writing about beings that are figments of fertile imaginations.

I should note one more thing about angels—the Bible divides them into two groups: the holy angels of God who do his bidding and the angels who followed Satan as he rebelled against God. The number of evil angels are said to have been about one-third of the total. Therefore, good angels are twice as numerous and by inference twice as powerful as the messengers of evil. That is a truth not told by many so-called "angel guides." In fact, they may lead you into an encounter with an "angel" who is out to destroy you! This is the reason why the Word of God is so important. Your knowledge of God's Word will be your best protection against the deceptions of Satan or any of his evil angels.

As you read any of the encounters in this book, measure them against the sure and truthful Word of God. Discipline yourself to be discerning in this area.

Please join me as we explore more exciting angelic adventures! Many of the truths contained in these stories are some you already know, but they may well be a reminder. Enjoy the journey! Read these stories through the eyes of people just like you who have been so privileged as to have had an angelic encounter. And if you are a person who has experienced angelic experiences, why not share it with me or with others. Your story may be the blessing and encouragement somebody else needs!

Robert J. Strand
Springfield, Missouri
2006

"My God sent his angel, and he shut the
mouths of the lions. They have not hurt me, because I
was found innocent in his sight. Nor have I ever done
any wrong before you, O King."
—*Daniel 6:22*

Chapter 1

A SHOCKING TIME AT THE BOARDING SCHOOL

In the following story, Henrietta W. Romman shares an incredible incident that happened when she was eleven years old in her hometown of Khartoum in Africa:

My mom, Juliette, was extremely ill with asthma, which had already affected her heart. It became necessary for her to travel to Egypt for essential treatment, but my parents weren't sure what to do with us five children during that time.

The only solution they could arrive at was that my two younger sisters would go with them, while my two brothers and I would remain safely in Khartoum as boarders in our familiar school premises. Henry and Charles were to stay in the boarding house of the Comboni Catholic School for boys while I was to stay in the same school's boarding house for girls, which was located in the adjoining building.

Our parents left and I began my temporary living arrangements among twenty-five other girls—some were my age and a few were older. Although this took place during the summer vacation, we were still supervised by our school teacher nuns. It was a wonderful time of play, completing interesting projects, and just being children in the playground. We felt safe and secure under the watchful eyes of the friendly and loving nuns.

As the newcomer, I was privileged to use the separate, beautiful guest bathroom. This particular building was rarely used, and so the electrical system had not been checked recently.

Being eleven years old, I felt joyful and highly favored. On the first afternoon at shower time, I entered the bathroom with the necessary change of clothing. After I had showered, I proceeded to dry myself and my hair with a thin towel until the poor thing was soaking wet.

Upon leaving, I proceeded to turn off the lights. I made a half turn with the wet towel between my right-hand forefinger and thumb, and reached for the light switch with the same hand. Unfortunately, I didn't just flick the switch but held it and slowly turned it.

What happened next was totally unexpected! My hand stuck to the light switch, and electrical shocks ran through my body with such an intensity that I began to shake and scream: "AH . . . AHHHH . . . A . . . A . . . A . . . Ah! A . . . A . . . A . . . Ahhh!

All my energy and my life quickly drained from my body. I knew I would soon die, and no one would know about it for hours. My mind went blank. I couldn't let loose and continued to shake and moan.

Instantly, out of nowhere, the tall and graceful Sister Maria Questanca, my previous year's teacher, drifted into the room so quietly, grabbed me around the waist, and quickly snatched me away from the light switch. Sorella Maria, as we girls called her, gently carried me over to a nearby chair.

When I thanked my rescuer, she never said a word but simply checked me over to make sure I was all right, and then left. I felt so safe and relaxed that I closed my eyes and dozed off to sleep.

Later some girls came and roused me for supper. When I described to them what had just taken place in the bathroom, they were astounded. I told them of the nun's role in saving my life.

"Girls," I shared, "I never knew she was so beautiful, and so kind and so quiet!"

At these words, my friends looked at each other perplexed, and I heard one of them exclaim, "But she is in Italy to visit the Pope!" Another girl asked, "Do you think the electricity spoiled her mind?" One other girl added, "She is imagining strange things."

At their words, I asked, "If this was not the real nun who helped me, then who was she?"

If you make the Most High your dwelling—even the Lord, who is my refuge—then no harm will befall you, no disaster will come near your tent. For He will command His angels concerning you to guard you in all your ways; they will lift you up in their hands, so that you will not strike your foot against a stone. You will tread upon the lion and the cobra; you will trample the great lion and the serpent (Psalm 91:9-13).

FOOD FOR THOUGHT: One of the ministries of angels is to provide protection over believers and children. And the above biblical passage is an example of the fulfillment of a promise of angelic protection to us as God's people. Reread the above scriptural passage. What promises are made that you can claim for divine protection today for your situation?

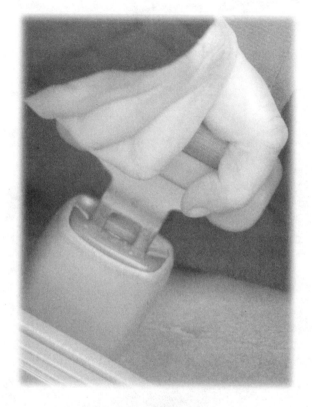

"O Lord Almighty,
blessed is the man who
trusts in You."
—*Psalm 84:12*

Chapter 2

AN ANGEL
WITH A LOUD VOICE

Debra Weber of Springfield, Missouri, is a busy lady—she is a mother of three, wife to a busy husband, schoolteacher, and volunteer. She's a woman with lots of things on her mind.

On this particular day, Debra had to run an errand. She was in a hurry and jumped in the car, barreled down the street, and moved into heavier traffic. Then she heard a gentle voice say: "Debra, put on your seat belt." Although this was her normal routine, she had forgotten to do it when she had started the car; looking at the cars around her, she didn't think she could take her hands off the wheel to do it now. Busy with watching traffic, she promptly forgot about the command, unusual though the voice was.

About two minutes later the voice came again, this time so loud and so forceful it shook the car: "DEBRA, PUT ON YOUR SEAT BELT!"

This time she pulled over and quickly obeyed the voice. She thought, *This is most unusual; where did this voice come from? Am I hearing things or did it really happen?*

Less than five minutes later, as she was moving through a major intersection with the light in her favor, an out-of-control car ran the red light and plowed directly into the passenger side of her car. It demolished her car, but there was not a scratch on Debra.

As she related the story to me she asked, "Okay, how do you explain it? I didn't see anything, but I sure heard it."

I had no quick and sure explanation. I just shrugged my shoulders, and she declared, "I believe it was an angel with a loud voice!"

In our last story, there was an appearance in which the angel didn't say a word. But in this story, an angel spoke gently in an audible voice first and then later shouted to finally get Debra's attention. How do you explain it?

Do we really need to have a plausible explanation before we become believers? Not everything can be explained by human reasoning. In the spiritual world we are told to be believers and accept some things in faith at face value.

Most of us experience the quiet leading of the Spirit in our lives based on the instructions of God's Word, but at critical times there is a need for the spectacular intervention by angels. Thank God He can work in both ways in our lives!

But after he had considered this, an angel of the Lord appeared to him in a dream and said, "Joseph son of David, do not be afraid to take

Mary home as your wife, because what is conceived in her is from the Holy Spirit. She will give birth to a son, and you are to give him the name Jesus, because he will save his people from their sins" (Matthew 1:20-21).

FOOD FOR THOUGHT: There you have it—a biblical setting in which an angel gave specific instructions to Joseph. So why couldn't there be an angel in a car in the twenty-first century? What should the response be to Debra's question? Was it the voice of an angel? Was it a genuine angelic message? How did Joseph know it was a real, genuine message in his life? How will you know if it's a genuine angelic message or some kind of an imaginative fantasy? The simple test is: Does it match up with biblical truth?

"Angels, where ere we go,
Attend our steps whate'er betide.
With watchful care their charge attend,
And evil turn aside."
—*Charles Wesley*

Chapter 3

DEBRA'S ANGELIC
PROTECTION

Debra had become desperately sick—so ill that she slipped into a coma, which lasted a number of days. After her recovery she recounted the following incident:

In the middle of her coma, in her mind, in her dream, in her vision—you pick which one—Debra vividly saw a bright, beautiful being who appeared to be made of light. This being was beyond description. Then he spoke, "Stay with your boys; we don't need you here now!" Then he just disappeared, and she came out of her coma and made a complete recovery.

Her husband, Tim, who was at her bedside when this incident happened, saw her reach both hands heavenward in an act of worship or acceptance. It was at that point when she opened her eyes.

You know you can pick such events all to pieces by attempting to apply logical thinking to them. You can explain them away, but to the people who experience them, like Debra, you can't take away the experience.

Debra has yet one more fascinating story:

For a little more than six years she was commuting from Springfield to the neighboring town of Republic to fulfill her responsibilities as a schoolteacher. The road she always took is a four-lane highway with turn lanes and stoplights.

She was stopped in the middle lane between the right-hand car and one in the left turn lane, waiting for the light to change. Barreling toward the intersection, as the light changed to red, was a bright red out-of-control fully loaded eighteen-wheeler! It smashed into the car that had been in the turn lane making a left turn and then into a second car. The truck tipped on its side, pushing the two cars ahead of it, and skidded at a high rate of speed directly toward Debra and her car!

It seemed like there was nothing she could do but prepare for the crash. And so she did. She shouted, "Jesus! Make it stop!"

All of a sudden there was an appearance of a huge hand between Debra and the oncoming truck pushing the smashed cars toward her. Then the strangest, most wonderful thing happened. This smashed-up mess—two cars and a semi with its trailer—came to an absolute halt not more than three or four inches from her car! Gas and oil spills were covering the highway, making fire a real possibility. She scrambled out of her car, ran to the shoulder out of harm's way, and stood there giving praise to God for protection.

How had it happened? The truck driver had fallen asleep at the wheel and lost control. The highway patrol quickly arrived on the scene and took it all in. The policeman spoke to Debra, "Lady, it is some kind of a miracle that you were not struck by the careening truck. I can't believe it. How did you survive?" So she recounted the events as she remembered them.

He then replied, "There is no other explanation for this truck coming to such a quick and sudden stop. Do the angels always ride with you?"

Oh, yes, I almost forgot. The two other car drivers and the truck driver all escaped injury; they were just shook up a bit. The patrolman could hardly believe his eyes and told Debra, "It is impossible to have such damage and no injuries. It had to be some kind of divine interference."

Suddenly an angel of the Lord appeared and a light shone in the cell. He struck Peter on the side and woke him up. "Quick, get up!" he said, and the chains fell off Peter's wrists. Then Peter came to himself and said, "Now I know without a doubt that the Lord sent his angel and rescued me from Herod's clutches and from everything the Jewish people were anticipating" (Acts 12:7, 11).

FOOD FOR THOUGHT: Angels are beings of action! One struck Peter and, if I know Peter, he was probably a deep sleeper. He woke Peter and commanded, "Quick! Get up!" Their actions can happen quickly. Intervention can happen in mere seconds. Now that thought is incredible. How can they get from heaven to earth and know their orders in less time than it takes to tell this story? Maybe someday we will be privileged to understand.

"The angels are the dispensers and
administrators of the divine beneficence toward us;
they regard our safety, undertake our defense,
direct our ways, and exercise a constant
solicitude that no evil befall us."
— *John Calvin*

Chapter 4

THE ART OF FLYING

The following is a story coming to us out of the early days of World War II. It was a time in history when England's air force saved their nation from invasion by the German army and what looked to be imminent defeat.

Adela Rogers St. John, in her book *Tell No Man,* recounts a strange and interesting aspect of a week-long air war. She cites information that came from a celebration honoring Air Chief Marshal Lord Hugh Dowding, which took place some months after the war was over.

The king of England, the prime minister, and scores of government and military dignitaries were present. In his remarks, Dowding told the story of the legendary conflict when his pitifully small complement of men rarely slept. He told of their planes being refueled and re-armed and immediately put back up into the skies. He also shared stories about pilots on their missions who were hit and were either dead or incapacitated, yet their planes kept flying and fighting!

Dowding said that it happened frequently, and there were times when other pilots in other planes were able to see a figure at the controls that enabled the crew to continue the fighting. Sometimes when a plane landed at the base, the pilot was found disabled or even dead!

How do you explain this? The air chief marshal said he believed angels had actually flown some of the planes when the pilots sat dead in their cockpits!

Fabulous! How can we prove this? I must confess that I can't prove it and neither could Dowding. But he believed it, and the only way those planes could have landed was through a supernatural intervention! He believed there were angels helping in the affairs of men.

Would angels help us fight a war today? Maybe you're not like me, but when I write about such things, I always seem to come away with more questions than answers. How about you? At the bottom line, we need to take the story at face value and believe in faith that it really did happen.

Then, again, as you read the Bible, especially in the Old Testament, you will discover any number of incidents in which angels were involved in fighting a war, destroying an enemy of the people of God, or winning a victory for the people who worshiped God.

The Bible dramatically pictures how angels have taken an active part in fighting a war. King Hezekiah had received a letter from the commander of the Assyrian forces and had immediately sought the counsel of God. God gave Isaiah a promise: not one Assyrian arrow would be fired into the city of Jerusalem! Furthermore, God said He would defend Jerusalem for His servant David's sake. That night, just one angel—yes, one angel—struck the Assyrian camp, and the next morning 185,000 soldiers were found dead!

Therefore this is what the Lord says concerning the king of Assyria: "He will not enter this city or shoot an arrow here. He will not come before it with shield or build a siege ramp against it. By the way that he came he will return; he will not enter this city, declares the Lord. I will defend this city and save it, for my sake and for the sake of David my servant." That night the angel of the Lord went out and put to death a hundred and eighty-five thousand men in the Assyrian camp . . . (2 Kings 19:32-35).

FOOD FOR THOUGHT: There's no reason why angels could not have helped in the saving of Great Britain against the onslaught of the Nazi Luftwaffe. After all, it would seem angels know quite a bit about the art of flying!

"All God's angels
come to us
disguised."
—*James Russell
Lowell*

Chapter 5

NO SUCH ADDRESS

Ioften marvel at the great variety of angel stories
people have shared with me. Some border on the edge
of being totally unbelievable were it not for the supernatural element that makes them possible. Russell F.
DeHart of Fruita, Colorado, shares such a story:

We were driving through Arizona on our way back
home from a family vacation in California. The family
had quieted down and everyone was either asleep or
very nearly there. It was a calm, clear, hot night in
Arizona. I preferred to cover some of this stretch of
highway at night because of the intense heat during the
day. Things were going along nicely when I noticed the
temperature gauge on the dashboard begin to rise. Soon
it was indicating an overheating engine, and we needed
help quickly.

Fortunately, I managed to get the car to the next exit
where there happened to be a small mini-mart and com-
bination gas pump. I pulled in and inquired about some
help. The attendant assured me there would be no help
until morning anywhere in the area, and furthermore he

didn't know of any nearby mechanics. It was a pretty remote location with the next service station miles away.

All of a sudden, a man stepped up from an aisle in the store. I hadn't noticed anybody else around when I entered the store and didn't know how or when he could have made his appearance. The store attendant seemed also surprised to see someone else in the store. This strange man asked me what was wrong.

I replied, "My car is overheating and I'm not quite sure what is wrong. I need to get it to a mechanic or a garage for some help."

He said, "Well, just follow me to my house. I'll give you some help. It's not far, just a couple of blocks, and I'm sure it won't hurt your car to drive such a short distance."

I really had no other choice. He seemed to be a nice man, but you know how it is when you're away from home and in a strange place with strange people, but I followed him despite my fears.

We pulled up into his driveway, and he went for some tools. In a very quick time, our car was fixed. He produced some antifreeze to replace the coolant I had lost, and we were ready to get underway again. I was surprised at how little time it had taken. I attempted to pay the man for his time and materials, but he absolutely refused to take anything.

As we drove out of his place, we took down the address and house number from his mailbox as well as his name. After we arrived home, I sent him a special "thank you" card and more than enough money to cover his costs. In a few days the note was returned and marked: "No such person known" and "No such address."

We were puzzled, but thought no more about it. A few months later we had to make another quick trip to California and pass through this same town. We decided to take the note and the money, and track down this helpful stranger.

We drove into town and began looking for the house. We found the street but could not find the house or house number. We inquired down at the courthouse, showing them the name and the house number. The clerk replied, "No such person has ever lived in this town, and there has never been a house built at the address you have given me!"

Russell said in recounting the story, "I firmly believe this man was an angel sent to help us."

> *Are not all angels ministering spirits sent to serve those who will inherit salvation?* (Hebrews 1:14).

FOOD FOR THOUGHT: I love the word picture painted here by the writer of the Book of Hebrews—angels are ministering spirits. A "ministering" being is one who attends to needs, serves, answers, obliges, tends, and takes care of someone in need. Awesome!

"While we do not place our
faith directly in angels, we should place it
in the God who rules the angels;
then we can have peace."
—*Billy Graham*

Chapter 6

WHAT BIG GUY?

This happened on an Indian reservation in the state of North Dakota. A man we'll call Marvin Ellsworth is the pastor of an Indian mission church on the reservation.

The day started out like any other day on the North Dakota prairie—a bit on the windy side, but a clear and bright, sunny summer day. Suddenly an Indian boy about fifteen or sixteen came running down the road toward the mission. Pastor Ellsworth looked out the window and went outside to meet the boy. He was out of breath but managed to get out the news that a fight had broken out between two factions.

The pastor asked, "Did you call the sheriff?"

The boy replied, "Yes, but he is out on another call and can't come."

Again the pastor asked, "Have you asked anybody else for help?"

"No."

"Well, how many are involved?"

"About thirty or thirty-five people."

There was nobody else to quiet things down, so the pastor said, "Come with me," as he quickly ran to the van.

When the two of them drove up to where the men were fighting, Pastor Ellsworth quickly sized up the situation. They were all armed with baseball bats, knives, clubs, lead pipes, and guns. The situation was not good, and fear gripped the pastor. He quickly said a fervent prayer for protection and stepped out of the van. The fighting immediately stopped, and all combatants turned their attention toward the pastor.

He said, "I spoke for about twenty minutes. I thought it was probably the best sermon I have ever preached. I said things but wasn't sure where they came from. I quoted scripture I didn't even know. And they all stood completely focused on me, still holding their weapons. They didn't pay any attention to each other or who their enemy was. The longer I spoke, the bolder I felt. When I finished speaking, quietly each of the combatants made their way to their cars or pickups and drove off. There was no more fighting or even taunts. And you can only guess at how relieved I felt.

"I noticed that the two leaders started talking to each other and motioned at me. I began to feel fear gripping my heart. These guys were big, much larger than I am. They slowly began walking toward me. I didn't know whether to run or jump in my van and attempt a quick getaway or what. I just froze in apprehension as they came closer. Both were armed, and neither smiled or showed any emotion. But they kept on slowly moving in my direction.

"They stopped about three feet in front of me. I was cornered with my back against my van and the two of them on each side of me. I looked from one to the other. Then one of the leaders spoke, 'Tell us who the great big guy is who stood behind you while you were speaking and is now standing over there.'

"I whirled around to look but couldn't see any big guy, but these two faction leaders clearly saw him. Then it dawned on me—God had sent a guardian angel!"

This particular incident marked the beginning of many good things at the church mission. Barriers were broken and many of the Native Americans began attending the church with the pastor who had the "big guy" for protection!

> *"Don't be afraid," the prophet answered. "Those who are with us are more than those who are with them." And Elisha prayed, "O Lord, open his eyes so he may see." Then the Lord opened the servant's eyes, and he looked and saw the hills full of horses and chariots of fire all around Elisha (2 Kings 6:16-17).*

FOOD FOR THOUGHT: Angelic protection is a constant theme running through many of these stories. We have been taught about "guardian" angels and that each of us, especially children, have one. One premise for the guardian angel is based on the statement of Jesus in

Matthew 18:10, "See that you do not look down on one of these little ones. For I tell you that their angels in heaven always see the face of my Father in heaven." What a comforting concept—a special guardian on duty 24/7 for us!

"For God will deign
To visit oft the dwellings of just men
Delighted, and with frequent intercourse
Thither will send his winged messengers
On errants of supernal grace."
—*John Milton*

Chapter 7

AN ANGEL FOR AN ANGELL

Hi, my name is Angell, Judith Angell," she said as she introduced herself to me. We had stopped at a craft and gift shop in one of Missouri's top tourist spots. I couldn't believe my ears.

"Would you be so kind as to repeat that?" I asked.

"Sure," she said, with a smile this time. "My name is Judith Angell."

I was intrigued because I'm always on the lookout for another angel story worth sharing with my readers. And it's amazing where these stories have come from and how they have been shared and eventually end up in print.

So I pressed on, "Surely there's some kind of an angel story connected with you and a name like that."

She smiled some more and replied, "Yes, I get asked something like that all the time. Why do you ask?"

"I'm a writer and I'm always on the alert for another story for the next book I have been commissioned to write about angel encounters," was my answer.

"Well, what kind of a book are you writing?"

"This is the third in the series of stories. In fact, I've just done a book-signing in the area and happen to have a sample. If you'll wait, I'll run out to the car and show you the format and leave a copy with you." I brought back my book *Angel at My Door* and discussed what I need to have in an angel story.

To which she replied, "Okay, I'll share it." And she proceeded to tell me the following story.

This story happened just a few short days ago. I have worked all over the world with a major investment company and took an early retirement. I'm single so I can live almost any place in the world, but I chose this area and bought myself a working horse ranch. I raise registered horses and train them. It's something I've always wanted to do, and I found the exact ranch I desired.

One day, as I looked over my yearling herd, I couldn't find a particular stallion. He was missing, and I immediately became alarmed. So I set out on foot looking for him in the pasture where he was supposed to be. Now my ranch covers more than a thousand acres so this could be a long search. I made my way to the very back of the ranch and found him tangled up in the fence! When he saw me, he whinnied and looked at me with fear in his eyes. Somehow he had managed to get both front feet tangled up in the barbed-wire fence.

By this time I was a long way from my barns, house, and help. It would take me more than an hour to go for help and return. Fortunately, he was standing quietly, not moving, but you could see where the barbs had ripped into his legs, and the blood was dripping. I just sat down in frustration and began to cry. What could I do? Who would help? If I left him, would he injure himself more? Would he panic if I left? Would he struggle?

All of a sudden I heard a voice, "Judith, get up!" I looked around, but nobody could be seen. Was I hearing things? Then again I heard, "Judith, get up!" and it was louder this time. I was really thinking that I might be losing it, so I still sat there. Once more, "JUDITH, GET UP!" This time I obeyed, but I wasn't sure what to do.

Then came further instructions, "Get under the horse and lift up his front legs, and you will get him out of the fence." So I scrambled under him, placed my head between his two front legs, and began to lift up against his chest. Now when you think about this, it's ridiculous. There I was, a woman in my early sixties, not weighing more than 110 pounds, attempting to lift a nearly full-grown horse! But as I straightened my back and lifted upward holding his two legs with my hands, he came loose and was suddenly freed! I dropped to my hands and knees while he stood still and then I crawled out from under him.

Where had the voice and the instructions come from? The only conclusion I have is that an angel came to my rescue! The little stallion? He quickly recovered with no scars or lasting injuries.

The angel of the Lord asked him, "Why have you beaten your donkey these three times? . . . The donkey saw me and turned away from me these three times . . ." (Numbers 22:32-33).

FOOD FOR THOUGHT: Do you think the Lord is interested enough in an animal to send an angel to help with the rescue? Why not? An angel was totally involved with the prophet Balaam and his donkey in the above scripture. Why not read the entire incident as found in Numbers 22:21-41?

"O welcome,
pure-eyed Faith,
white-handed Hope,
Thou hovering angel,
girt with golden wings!"
—*John Milton*

Chapter 8

THE BLACK-HAIRED
MESSENGER

Some angel stories have almost become legends in their retelling. The following, or something similar, has been shared with me more than once, but the conclusion is worth the read.

This story took place in Montana in the winter of 1898. Dr. Karl Muller had begun a practice in Billings in 1895 and was the only doctor for about five hundred miles around. Understandably, he was a busy man.

On this particularly cold and rainy night, there was a knock on his door. He opened it to find a thin little girl with rain-drenched black hair. Her clothes were soaked, and she wore a flimsy coat that didn't offer any help against the wet and cold. He invited her in, offered her dry clothes, and urged her to sit by the fire to warm up. She refused it all.

"There isn't time, doctor," came her reply. "My mother is very sick. She needs help soon or she will die. Please, come with me now."

Dr. Muller had the hired man hitch up his buggy

while he retrieved his black bag. Soon the doctor and the little girl rode away into the darkness. Before long, the doctor was shivering from the cold, but the little girl seemed unaffected by being wet or the frigid air. They came around a small hill and saw a covered wagon stuck in the mud with a lamp glowing on the inside. "Is that your wagon?" asked the doctor.

"Yes," said the little girl. "It got stuck in the mud, and my father went for help many hours ago. He must be lost. My mother is sick. Please hurry."

The doctor stopped the buggy, grabbed his black bag, and called out so as not to frighten the woman inside. He found a woman in her late twenties who was quite ill, clearly near death. Working quickly he did what he could, and the time passed until her fever broke near daylight. She finally was resting peacefully as the doctor climbed out of the wagon. It was still cold but at least the rain had stopped.

As the doctor was about to climb into his buggy, the husband came riding up, holding a rifle in his hands. "Who are you?"

"I'm Dr. Muller from Billings," he replied, as he eyed the rifle and the man. Then he continued, "She's had a rough time of it, but the fever has broken and she will be all right. All she needs is a few days of rest."

Relief showed on the rancher's face, as he dropped the rifle and began to cry. "Thank God," he sobbed. "I was lost in search of help but could find no one. I prayed for God to come and help my sick wife. I didn't think he had heard my prayer, but I returned and found you." He came over and hugged the doctor.

The doctor patted him on the back and said, "If it

hadn't been for your little daughter and her persistence, I would not have been here."

Stunned, the husband stepped back, "What are you talking about?"

Dr. Muller went through the events of the night and looked around to find the little girl, but she was nowhere to be seen. He noticed the thin little coat she had been wearing on the buggy seat. He held it out to the husband and said, "I don't know where she has gone, but here's her coat."

With shaking hands the man took the coat, held it, and cried again. "Doctor, this is her coat all right, but our little raven-haired daughter died two months ago. We buried her alongside the trail in Wyoming."

When the wife recovered and heard the story, she was convinced the black-haired visitor was an angel in disguise who had brought the doctor. The couple presented the coat to the doctor as a gift to remember this night.

The doctor moved to San Francisco in 1901, married, and had two daughters of his own. When they were older, he told them the story of the black-haired little girl with the thin coat. Today, according to the legend, the coat is in the possession of Dr. Muller's granddaughter who also plans to pass the story and coat on to her daughter!

When the water in the skin was gone, she put the boy under one of the bushes. Then she went off and sat down nearby . . . for she thought, "I cannot watch the boy die." And as she sat there nearby, she began to sob. God heard the boy crying, and the angel of God called to Hagar from heaven and said to her, "What is the matter, Hagar? Do not be afraid; God has heard the boy crying as he lies there. Lift the boy up and take him by the hand, for I will make him into a great nation" (Genesis 21:15-18).

FOOD FOR THOUGHT: "God has heard the boy crying as he lies there." Do you think God hears when we are in need and cry out for help? The story from Montana, as well as the biblical account of Hagar and Ishmael, should give us our answer in the positive! In other places God has encouraged us to "Call unto Me . . ." Are you in need? There's your invitation!

"Millions of spiritual
creatures walk the earth unseen,
both when we wake and
when we sleep."
—*John Milton*

Chapter 9

OH NOOOOO!

Junetta Fields of Kansas City, Missouri, had a very strange experience. Let's let her tell it in her own words:

A year ago, as was my habit, I went to bed about 10:00 p.m. Everything seemed to be normal. There was nothing out of the regular routine to indicate to me that this night would hold something strange. I fell asleep as usual.

About 2:00 a.m., I was awakened, but at first I didn't open my eyes. The strangest sensation began—it was as though I was dying. It seemed as if my breath was being drawn out of my body. It's difficult to put it into words. My breath was being drawn out of my body and suspended just out of reach of my arms. Air was steadily being sucked out of my lungs. It was as if an evil presence was intent on taking my life. I just knew I was dying.

But I also remember thinking, "If this is what it is like to die, this is not too bad. It's quite pleasant."

More time went by and the drawing away of my breath continued. Then I thought to myself, *I am not supposed to be dying because I haven't done what I was put on this earth to accomplish.*

And all the while my breath was being taken away, and I sensed the end was quite near. I was about to pass out and enter eternity when all of a sudden I realized there were two angels near my head—one on each side. I sensed their presence, opened my eyes, and saw two bright beings. I was sure they were angels sent on a mission. I just knew it in my mind and spirit.

One turned in my direction and said, "Oh, no!" It was emphatically said, but it was also drawn out and sounded something like this, "Oohhhh, nooooo!" It was like a command as though this angel was making sure death did not come to me!

Immediately my breath came back into my body, and I was able to breathe normally once again. I was zapped back into my body. It had been a frightening experience, yet at the same time, not one to be fearful about.

During those moments it seemed to me as though the angels or my own guardian angel had forgotten to be on duty. It was as if he had been assigned to take care of me and protect me against the enemy of my soul who wanted to kill me, but for a short period of time he had been distracted. It seemed as though he had forgotten to watch over me and suddenly had remembered.

I began to praise and thank the good Lord for His mercy and deliverance. And I thought about this experience, how it happened and what it could have been about.

With the reassurance of the presence of the two angels, I went back to sleep and slept the night through like a baby. I awoke in the morning strangely energized and in the best health of my life. Not only had there been protection, but there was a refreshing to my spirit and body!

> *But even the archangel Michael, when he was disputing with the devil about the body of Moses, did not dare to bring a slanderous accusation against him, but said, "The Lord rebuke you!"* (Jude 9).

FOOD FOR THOUGHT: I am always fascinated at the great variety of angelic encounters. Junetta experienced something beyond the normal sleep most of us experience, and I think it was a look into the spiritual world. From the above verse we can see that the devil is on the alert, ready to snatch away any servant of the Lord he can. But notice, Michael and the Lord won out!

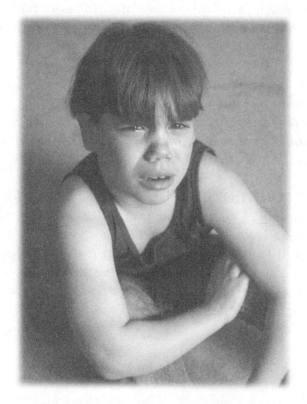

"Christians should never fail to sense
the operation of an angelic glory.
It forever eclipses the world
of demonic powers,
as the sun does
a candle's light."
—*Billy Graham*

Chapter 10

A WHOLE BUNCH OF ANGELS

Evelyn Niemeyer, a farm wife who lived near Fort Dodge, Iowa, had an interesting experience around 1979. She and her family had traveled to a Bible camp in Hungry Horse, Montana, for an annual camp meeting.

Herb Mjored, a Norwegian, was the man in charge of the camp as well as all the services. He was a dynamic worship leader as he led the attendees in their singing and worship. It always was an exciting gathering for Evelyn and her family. There were many different activities for all ages during the day, but everyone was in attendance for the evening services.

On this particular night the singing and worship were lively and spirited. At one point in the service, a lady stood up. When she was recognized by Herb, she asked, "May I say something?"

Herb replied, "Yes, go ahead."

She continued, "You know, I sense something very special—a special presence of the Lord in this place tonight. I just wish to express my praise and thanksgiving for this visitation." Then she sat down.

Almost instantly, a little boy about ten years of age stood up. He was crying and weeping so hard he couldn't be understood. Herb waited patiently, as did the congregation, and finally he regained his composure enough to say, "Many, many . . . I see hundreds of angels with us!"

The crowd was touched and rejoiced at this report. No one else saw any angels this night, but this short expression transformed the service. It was one of the most exciting and outstanding nights of worship and praise at the camp meeting for a number of years.

Evelyn concludes, "It struck me as being most unusual for a young child among adults to stand up and say what he said."

That brings to mind a question. Do angels "sing" or make up some kind of special "choir"? I know that authors and songwriters have depicted angels as singing. In fact, they have done such a good job until it is common knowledge that angels are always singing or playing a harp. Yes, I can find a place where Gabriel blows a trumpet, but it is a trumpet of judgment. But I can't find any place in the Bible where angels are shown to be singing!

The event most often depicted as an angelic choir is when the angels appeared to the shepherds at the birth of Jesus. But here's what the Bible says, "Suddenly a great company of the heavenly host appeared with the angel, praising God and *saying*, 'Glory to God in the highest, and on earth peace to men on whom his favor rests'" (Luke 2:13-14). Maybe this is a minor point of contention, but it illustrates how much wrong information there is out there in regard to angels and their ministry.

Now, if you think I am wrong, please contact me with the correct information that angels really do sing, but this information must be Bible based.

> *After this I heard what sounded like the roar of a great multitude in heaven SHOUTING: "Hallelujah!" . . . Then I heard what sounded like a great multitude, like the roar of rushing waters and like loud peals of thunder, SHOUTING: "Hallelujah! . . ."* (Revelation 19:1, 6; emphasis mine).

FOOD FOR THOUGHT: How did we end up here with a bit of controversy? I remind you again, what you hear about angels and angelic appearances should always be measured against the true Word of God, the Bible. If it doesn't pass the biblical test, don't accept it!

"An angel is a spiritual
creature created by God without
a body for the service of
Christendom and
the church."
—*Martin Luther*

Chapter 11

WARNINGS ABOUT ANGELS

During one of the most difficult times in her life, Donna had something happen to her that was so comforting. It happened during the time when she had been named in a multimillion-dollar lawsuit. Jess, who happened to be the church janitor, called her aside after a prayer time.

Jess said, "I need to tell you this. As you stood praying, I looked in your direction and saw angels over your head and all around you. Some were just standing there, while others were laughing and laughing. And still others were dancing! However, all of them were rejoicing and praising God."

That's quite a thought! And I'm sure it ministered life to Donna.

But perhaps this is a good point in the book to lay down a few guidelines or principles to serve as warnings as you continue your avid interest in angels.

The First Warning: WE MUST NOT RE-CREATE OR MAKE ANGELS AS WE WANT THEM TO BE. When it comes to the real spiritual reality, including angels, there is only one authority—the Bible! The majority of angels depicted today in paintings, gift books, lapel pins, and T-shirts are simply the result of a fertile imagination. Such depictions could be called fairy tales or phantoms, which might be closer to the truth.

Furthermore, gender or even race can be an issue. Whenever the Bible refers to angels, it's always in the masculine. The Bible never mentions a female angel even though some people have claimed to see a female angel. In fact, I have included an angel story with a little girl being seen as an angel. Angels are created beings; boys and girls do not become angels! Nor do angels indwell you; nor do they age. At times they may take on the *appearance* of a human—male or female—but they do not *become* human. Be on guard for the reworking of angels in today's world. Trust the Bible!

The SECOND Warning: DON'T ALLOW YOUR FASCINATION WITH ANGELS TO REPLACE GOD IN YOUR LIFE! *Christianity Today* made this statement: "Angels too easily provide a temptation for those who want a 'fix' of spirituality without bothering with God Himself."

And Professor Robert Ellwood, who is a specialist in unorthodox religions at UCLA, wrote: "With angels around, people feel they don't have to bother an Almighty God in order to get help."

Whenever you prefer angels over God—who is *their* Creator as well as being *our* Creator—it becomes an insult. Tragedy and spiritual shipwreck can happen quickly when people look for spiritual help from any other source than God.

In fact, the first two of the Ten Commandments carry warnings about worshiping anything or anyone other than God: You shall have no other gods before Me! You shall not make for yourself an idol!

The THIRD Warning: ANGELS MUST NEVER BE WORSHIPED! When you worship any other being, you can well expect to meet the devil who delights in coming to your party dressed up as an angel of light! The Bible is absolutely clear about this. Do not let anyone who delights in false humility and the worship of angels disqualify you for the prize (Colossians 2:18). They exchanged the truth of God for a lie, and worshiped and served created things rather than the Creator who is forever praised. Amen (Romans 1:25).

Even John, the writer of Revelations, was impressed enough by angels to fall down and worship them. But here's the response:

At this I fell at his feet to worship him. But he [the angel] said to me, "Do not do it! I am a fellow servant with you and with your brothers who hold to the testimony of Jesus. Worship God! For the testimony of Jesus is the spirit of prophecy" (Revelation 19:10).

There you have it—directly from the mouth of an angel. DO NOT WORSHIP ANGELS! WORSHIP GOD ALONE!

You guide me with your counsel, and afterward you will take me into glory. WHOM HAVE I IN

53

HEAVEN BUT YOU? And earth has nothing I desire besides you. My flesh and my heart may fail, but God is the strength of my heart and my portion forever! (Psalm 73:24-26; emphasis mine).

FOOD FOR THOUGHT: The following quote from A. W. Tozer says it better that I can: "Forever God stands apart, in light unapproachable. He is as high above an archangel as above a caterpillar; for the gulf that separates the archangel from the caterpillar is but finite, while the gulf between God and the archangel is infinite. The caterpillar and the archangel, though far removed from each other in the scale of created things, are nevertheless one in that they are alike created. They both belong in the category of that-which-is-not-God and are separated from God by infinitude itself."

"See, I am sending an
angel ahead of you to guard
you along the way . . ."
—*Exodus 23:20*

Chapter 12

FIRST INTO THE FIELD

It was springtime on the family fifteen-hundred-acre farm in North Dakota, and the oldest son, age fourteen, whom we'll call Eugene, was anxious to be the first farmer into the field in that area. Bragging rights were at stake. On this particular day school was out, and Eugene had begged his dad to let him be the first farmer out. He argued that it was dry enough. Finally his dad relented and said, "Okay, take the D-Case [which is a four-plow tractor] and the disc, and do the back eighty. But be careful."

Eugene was one happy young man! He worked until it was time to quit, then unhitched the disc and started out for home. He was standing up because the tractor had a hand clutch and it was easier to drive in that position. He was going at a wide open speed when he hit a dead furrow in the field. The tractor lurched and threw him off!

He flew over the steering wheel, landed in front of the right rear wheel, and attempted to get away, but the lugs on the tire caught his head and ran over it, mashing it into the newly turned earth. He was stunned but managed to get to his feet and run the quarter mile to the farm house, shouting as he banged open the door, "I've been run over by the tractor!"

His parents quickly got him into the car and sped toward town and the nearest hospital. The emergency room doctor took a quick look and asked what had happened. Eugene said, "I've been run over by the tractor." The doctor looked again and said, "No, you haven't."

But Eugene insisted and his parents backed him up. The doctor finally relented and took an X-ray. It showed multiple fractures of his skull and face. Then the doctor admitted him to a room, and the swelling began. Soon his head was bloated to about twice the normal size. The doctor then told his parents there was no chance Eugene would survive such injuries.

The pastor and their church were alerted, and everyone began to pray for Eugene. By the next evening, family members were assembled to say their last farewell to a dying son and brother. His head and face had turned black, his vital signs were slowing down, and he passed into a coma. The family members were all there, along with the pastor of their church. It was a solemn time as they prayed and waited. The doctors again assured the family that Eugene could not survive the night. He had been placed inside an oxygen tent to help with the breathing.

Suddenly Eugene sat up in the tent! He asked what day it was. Stunned, they replied, "March 29."

Eugene asked, "Why are all of you here?"

"Because we were told you were going to die tonight."

"That's funny; I feel great! I'm ready to go home and help you in the fields," he replied to his dad.

"How come you are feeling so great?" asked someone, not able to understand what was going on.

Eugene smiled through his swollen face, "Can't you see? There's an angel sitting on my bed, and he told me everything will be all right!" Nobody else in the room saw the angel, but the healing took place right before their eyes!

Eugene was completely healed with no complications and is alive and well today!

Are not all angels ministering spirits sent to serve those who will inherit salvation? (Hebrews 1:14).

FOOD FOR THOUGHT: Do angels have the power to heal someone? No! The power to heal comes from Jesus Christ and His sacrifice on Calvary, as it says "by His stripes we are healed." However, angels can well be the messengers of healing by carrying the good news that healing is taking place. Remember, angels are not the source of healing; God is!

"For he will command his
angels concerning you to guard
you in all your ways."
—*Psalm 91:11*

Chapter 13

A HIGHWAY ANGEL TO MY RESCUE—PART I

Vincent J. Kern of Snellville, Georgia, relates the following experience with an angel:

I'll never forget my encounter with an angel on a Saturday afternoon in mid-October 1979. Through divine intervention, the Lord sent an angel to save my life, an action I still think about now and again, and an encounter for which I shall be eternally grateful.

Due to the responsibilities associated with being an accountant (CPA), it was necessary for my employer to require the entire staff to work a fair amount of overtime during the year in order to meet quarterly and year-end tax filing deadlines. After putting in a good fifty-five hours of work for the week, I had decided to call it a day and drive to my home in Wilton, Connecticut. It was a gloomy, wet Saturday afternoon when I proceeded to make the routine half-hour commute back home.

While heading south on the Merritt Parkway, a two-lane highway in southwestern Connecticut, I decided to pass a slow moving vehicle that was traveling a good fifteen miles per hour less than the posted speed limit. I had just gotten parallel with the vehicle I was attempting to pass when my vehicle hit a large puddle forming on the low portion of the highway. Instantly I felt my car losing power and saw several red lights illuminate on my dashboard, indicating my car engine had shut down.

As my powerless 1972 Chevy Nova exited this large puddle and started up the next incline, I tried in vain to turn off the highway and park my dying car on the right-hand soft shoulder. Unfortunately, several vehicles in a row wouldn't permit me to pull back into the right lane, leaving me no alternative but to glide to a complete stop in the opposite lane of this two-lane highway.

Realizing the puddle had flooded my car's points and plugs, thereby causing the engine to shut off, I now sat at a complete stop in the left lane of a moderately traveled highway. Although I tried unsuccessfully to restart the car, it proved hopeless, so I turned on the four-way flashers and quickly jumped out of the car.

Fearing a possible collision, I stood on the very small left-hand shoulder, and motioned for approaching cars to pass my stalled car.

Sad to say, when many of the drivers saw me motioning them to move to the right, they decided to shout obscenities at me. After nearly thirty minutes of standing in the lightly falling rain and being maligned by strangers, my car's battery was growing very weak, causing the four-way flashers to cease.

At this point, I observed an older vehicle approaching the rear of my stalled car. I continued to motion the oncoming vehicle to pass my car but this vehicle continued to drive directly toward my car. At this point I thought the other car was on a collision course with my car, so I jumped over the guardrail to save my life. However, the driver slowed, stopped, rolled down the window, and told me he was going to help me.

As the man walked toward me, I'll never forget his appearance. He was clean shaven and appeared to be in his mid-thirties, with very light blue sparkling eyes, dark blond hair, and wearing a sport coat. He said to me, "We'll have to get your car over to the right-hand shoulder and out of the way of traffic."

I remember thinking to myself, "Right, Sherlock, how do you think we can push my stalled car up a hill and somehow stop all the oncoming traffic while we do this feat!"

Please read the next chapter for Part II and the rest of this story.

"Every redeemed one will understand
the ministry of angels in their own life. The
angel who was their guardian from their earliest
moment, the angel who watched their steps
and covered their head
in the day of peril."
— E. G. White

Chapter 14

A HIGHWAY ANGEL TO MY RESCUE—PART II

At this point, the clean-shaven man informed me he had a heavy chain in his car and he would pull me off the road. Within minutes, he pulled his car around to the front of mine. He attached the chain and told me to return to my car and successfully pulled my car over to the safety of the highway shoulder on the right side.

It didn't dawn on me until later that the entire time he was helping me, we had encountered no traffic coming from either direction! This was highly unlikely. Unusual, maybe even impossible!

Out of harm's way, he removed the chain. I attempted to start the car once more, but it was hopeless. He asked, "Is there anything else I can do to help you?"

"Yes," I replied. "Would you please drive me to the next exit so I could phone a friend who might be home to ask him to come and pick me up?" He obliged and within a couple of minutes we pulled up at a phone booth not far from the exit ramp.

As I was about to get out of his car, I noticed my newfound friend was soaking wet and his sport coat was a mess. I insisted that he take a twenty-dollar bill at the very least to cover the cost of dry-cleaning his coat. Three times I insisted, and each time he refused my small reward. I'll never forget the odd look on his face after rejecting my third offer for the money.

He looked directly at me with those piercing blue eyes as though he was looking right through me and said, "Don't thank me for being here, thank God for sending me to you."

His words caught me off guard, yet I knew he meant every word of it. With that I got out of the car and watched as he drove away—he and the car simply vanished. Gone. I could see down the highway about two or three miles, but he was long gone before he should have even reached the next curve.

I phoned my friend, who arrived shortly and drove us back to the stalled car. As he drove I briefly explained the afternoon's encounter, and he listened intently. At the disabled car, I figured I would make one final attempt to start it. When I opened the driver's door, I noticed the interior dome light was brightly lit. I turned the key in the ignition, and it immediately started. I glanced at the gauge on the dash to discover the previously dead battery was now fully charged! I had worked on a number of cars in the past and knew this was far from normal.

The story doesn't end here. During the next ten years I retold this story a handful of times to friends. Eight years later I sold my CPA practice and accepted a professional position in the Atlanta, Georgia, area.

Shortly after, I attended a church conference. While I was there, a middle-aged African-American man walked up to me, looked me in the eye and told me that there were three separate times in my life when the Lord had sent angels to protect me from imminent death by putting His hand of divine protection upon me.

Then he began to laugh! He continued, "The man who so graciously rescued you on the highway was an angel sent by God, and both God and the angel found it humorous when you attempted to offer an angel twenty dollars for his sport coat to be cleaned!"

Then this man disappeared. Because I had never seen him before and wanted to track him down to thank him for those words, I asked about him. It turned out that no one knew him, had seen him, or even knew where he could have come from!

I consider this to have been a direct confirmation from the Lord as to His divine intervention on my behalf. And He just might have sent another angel to share the message with me!

He holds victory in store for the upright, he is a shield to those whose walk is blameless, for he guards the course of the just and protects the way of his faithful ones (Proverbs 2:7-8).

FOOD FOR THOUGHT: What an amazing story! It's the last part that makes it different from many of the others we have read about help and deliverance. What a wonderful God! What a caring God who can and will send an angel to "guard the course of the just and protect the way" of His followers! What a word of assurance!

"Angels are unsatisfiable in their longing
to do by all means all manner of good unto
all the creatures, especially the
children of men."
—*Richard Hooker*

Chapter 15

ANGELS IN MEN'S CLOTHING

Henrietta W. Romman of Rogersville, Missouri, shares another of her experiences with us:

I shall recount a very recent encounter with angels in human form, dressed in modern clothes and behaving like most of us do.

We were among the crowds of people heading to their seats on September 13, 2003, in the Hammons Student Center auditorium, located on the campus of Southwest Missouri State University in Springfield, Missouri. This event occurred on the second day of the convention of a well-known evangelist.

My husband William and I had been quite positive such services were not for us, yet it had been arranged for us to attend. We felt our assignment was to do more than attend; we were to be in prayer for others who were in attendance.

When we arrived in the early afternoon, it was as though our seats had already been reserved for us. The ushers seated us on the first and only two seats available in a section. Immediately in front of us was an aisle about five yards wide. These happened to be the best seats in the house, and we could easily take in all the action.

After we sat down, William and I bent our heads and held hands as we began to pray for people who would be in need. After a bit, we opened our eyes and watched. Lots of people came by, all with something in their hands—something to drink, something to munch on, etc.—all except three young men who approached us empty-handed. The first one smiled beautifully at us. He was extremely tall, with blond hair and deep green eyes. I noticed his clothing—a blue shirt, denim jeans, and a denim jacket casually thrown over his left shoulder.

They came closer and the first one knelt on one knee so as to be at eye level with us. He reached out his hand and first greeted William and then held my hand. (It seemed as though this was happening away from the hustle and bustle of the auditorium, it was so quiet and peaceful.) He looked at us from one to the other. It was so strange. I attempted to introduce ourselves. He abruptly cut me short and exclaimed: "We know you! We want you to know that God loves you. God appreciates you. Your prayers are always heard. Listen! We are here to tell you that you are doing well in teaching the young people around you to be good apostles. But you both are meeting with much spiritual warfare, especially healthwise. Please look at the Word of God and carry on. Don't be afraid. Take heart in your work!"

Then he stood up. We stood up, and I almost shrieked at him, "What is your name?"

He looked as if searching for a name to end this encounter. Twice he uttered, "Steven, Steven."

Then with those same beautiful smiles, the three visitors continued on their way and swept past us. We keenly followed them for a second or two and then they quietly melted into thin air!

We looked at each other with our hearts beating fast. Our spirits were enriched and inspired. We looked around and asked the folks sitting next to us if they had just seen our three visitors. It turned out that no one else had seen them.

Then and there, because I am a writer and a columnist, I took out my notebook and wrote down every single word of the one-way communication from God's messengers sent to us. Then once more, together we bowed our heads reverently and prayed, "Thank You, Lord. Thank You for trusting us."

> *When I was a child, I talked like a child, I thought like a child, I reasoned like a child. When I became a man, I put childish ways behind me. Now we see but a poor reflection as in a mirror; then we shall see face to face. Now I know in part; then I shall know fully, even as I am fully known* (1 Corinthians 13:11-12).

FOOD FOR THOUGHT: Angels are sent to minister to us personally! Many biblical accounts assure us that we are the objects of their personal concern. In Martin Luther's book *Table Talk* he makes this statement: "An angel is a spiritual creature created by God without a body, for the service of Christendom and the church."

"Our forefathers went down into Egypt,
and we lived there many years. The Egyptians
mistreated us and our fathers, but when we cried
out to the Lord, he heard our cry and sent
an angel and brought us
out of Egypt . . ."
—*Numbers 20:15-16*

Chapter 16

THE BOOKSTORE ANGEL

Ruth Graham, wife of evangelist Billy Graham, relates this strange happening that took place in a Christian bookstore in Shanghai, China, in 1942. Her father, Dr. L. Nelson Bell, who served in the hospital in Tsingkiangpu, Kiangsu province, told the story.

The setting was the bookstore in which Dr. Bell bought his gospel portions and tracts to distribute among his patients. After the Japanese had taken control of much of China, they imposed their control on the Chinese. One morning, about nine o'clock, a Japanese truck stopped outside the bookstore. It was carrying five Japanese marines, and the truck was half-filled with books. The bookstore assistant, who happened to be alone in the store at this time, realized with dismay that they had come to confiscate his stock.

Jumping from the truck, the marines made for the bookstore door, but before they could enter, a neatly dressed Chinese gentleman came into the store ahead of them.

The shop assistant knew practically everybody who

frequented the store, but he did not know this stranger! For some unknown reason, the marines seemed unable to follow him into the store. They stood outside and milled around, looking in at the four large storefront windows. No one else was in the store and no one else outside, yet each time they attempted to enter the store they were unable to do so.

For a bit more than two hours they stood around, looking in but never setting foot inside. The well-dressed stranger asked what the soldiers wanted, and the assistant shopkeeper explained the Japanese had taken books from the other bookshops in the area and now wanted to take some from his bookstore.

The two prayed together and this stranger encouraged him, and so more than two hours passed. It was as though some kind of barrier had been placed across the entrance blocking their entry. At last the marines shook their heads, climbed back into their truck, and drove away.

Then the stranger also left. He had spent more than two hours in the store without making a single purchase. He had not even made an inquiry about any of the items in the store.

Later the same day, the bookstore owner, Mr. Christopher Willis (whose Chinese name was Lee), returned. The shop assistant asked, "Mr. Lee, do you believe in angels?"

"I do," replied Mr. Lee.

"So do I, Mr. Lee," said the assistant, who then told the storeowner the events of the morning.

Could this stranger have been one of God's protecting angels? Dr. Nelson Bell always thought so.

How about you? Do you believe in angels? It's quite likely you do or you would not be reading this book. Or maybe you are a person who is searching for answers, and you're looking for evidence that angels might be real. Believers accept the truth about angels by faith based on the teachings of God's Word.

> *The angel of the Lord found Hagar near a spring
> . . . that is beside the road to Shur* (Genesis
> 16:7).

FOOD FOR THOUGHT: Would the enemies, who attack Christians, be thwarted more if we grasped the concept that God's angels are on duty nearby to help in time of need? Interesting idea to think about.

"In old days there were angels who came
and took men by the hand and led them away
from the city of destruction. We see no
white-winged angels now. But yet men
are led away from threatening
destruction."
—*George Eliot*

Chapter 17

GOD, PLEASE PROTECT HIM

Jenean Franklin of Grand Junction, Colorado, shares a story of her family's history that is much too long to include here. All we really need to know for background is that her teenage son, Phyl, had given them lots of problems.

This story begins with seventeen-year-old Phyl spending some time with his grandparents. Jenean always prayed for God to send angels to protect Phyl wherever he happened to be and in whatever circumstances in which he might might find himself.

Phyl and some of his friends had been swimming by the Black Bridge over the Gunnison River in Colorado. They had been partying as well as drinking. There were more friends than could comfortably fit in their car, but they had only the one car.

Jenean begins her story:

My sister had taken my mom to pay some bills and on their way home passed a really bad accident. When they got home it was some time before my son came in. He showered and changed his clothes and started out the door when Grandma asked where he was going.

"My friends and I were in an accident and I have to go to the hospital. I was the only one who didn't get hurt," came the answer.

After more questioning, we discovered that, sure enough, it was the accident we had passed while returning home. No one had been killed, but the other six teens had all been injured seriously enough to spend some time in the hospital in recovery.

Then we discovered that Phyl had been the driver, and his head had broken through the windshield, along with his shoulders and upper torso. He had been able to pull himself back through the sharp edges of broken glass without a scratch or a bump on the head. There was absolutely no evidence of an accident on his body! The patrolman who was first on the accident scene just shook his head in amazement over Phyl's escape.

Jenean, to this day is absolutely convinced the injury-less accident to her wayward son was possible because of angelic protection. But why was he spared and none of the others? Would an angel or angels appear on the scene even if none of the passengers or the driver were wearing seat belts? Would an angel rescue a wayward teenager who had been drinking?

Lots of interesting questions come to mind, questions that have no easy answers. You could easily dismiss this story and explain it away with logic. It was a lucky break; it was a set of fortunate circumstances. But what about the fact that there was a mother who had prayed often and fervently for her wayward teen? This mother is absolutely convinced that Phyl's escape from injury was due to God's answer to her prayer for angelic protection.

> *The angel of the Lord encamps around those who fear him, and he delivers them. Taste and see that the Lord is good; blessed is the man who takes refuge in him* (Psalm 34:7-8).

FOOD FOR THOUGHT: What encouragement and what strength comes to the believer when contemplating this "divine surveillance"! God is watching; angels are watching and standing guard. The events of our lives are under scrutiny. These are factors in God's plan to promote and protect His people, and, sometimes, those who are not yet His people.

"Good news from heaven the angels bring,
Glad tidings to the earth they sing:
To us this day a child is given,
To crown us with the joy of heaven."
—*Martin Luther*

Chapter 18

I CAN FACE IT UNAFRAID!

A number of years ago, when we lived in Madison, Wisconsin, my wife Donna and I were privileged to travel to Milwaukee where we were part of a crowd that heard the late Corrie ten Boom. It took place in a theater, and we were seated about midway back in the center section. This is the story as I remember her telling it.

Together, Betsie (my sister) and I, along with the other women, were herded into a most terrifying building. It took place in the Ravensbrück Nazi prison camp. At the first table were women who took all our possessions. Everyone had to undress completely and then go into another room where our hair was checked.

I asked a woman who was busy checking the possessions of the new arrivals if I might use the toilet. She pointed to a door, and I discovered the toilet was just a hole in the shower-room floor. Betsie was with me all this time.

Suddenly I had a thought. "Quick, take off your woolen underwear," I whispered to her. I rolled it up with mine and laid the bundle in a corner along with my little Bible. The spot was alive with cockroaches, but I didn't worry about that. I felt strangely alive, relieved and happy. "The Lord is answering our prayers, Betsie," I whispered. "We shall not have to make the sacrifice of all our clothes."

We then hurried back to the line of women waiting to be undressed. Later, after we had our "de-lousing" showers and put on our shirts and shabby dresses, I hid the roll of underwear and my Bible under my dress. Obviously it did bulge out, but I prayed, "Lord, cause now your angels to surround me; and let them not be transparent today because the guards must not see me."

I felt perfectly at ease. Calmly I passed the guards. Everybody was being checked on all four sides, front and back and sides. Not a single bulge under our clothes got by the eyes of the guards. The woman in front of me had attempted to hide a warm woolen vest under her dress, and it was taken from her. They let me pass because they didn't see me. Betsie, behind me, was searched.

But it wasn't over yet. Outside we had another search, with more danger. On each side of the doorway were women who looked us over once more. This time they felt over the body of each one who passed. It was another thorough search.

I just knew they couldn't see me. I was calm. I knew the angels were still surrounding me. So I wasn't surprised when they passed me through. They searched the woman in front of me and Betsie in back of me, but didn't see me and so I passed through this search, too.

Inside of me rose up the jubilant cry of victory and deliverance, "O Lord, if Thou dost so answer my prayer, I can face even Ravensbrück unafraid!"

And she did! Her story is fabulous and faith building. I would encourage you, if you haven't already read it, to get her story in book form. You will be fascinated. It's a story of true deliverance.

> *For it seems to me that God has put us apostles on display at the end of the procession, like men condemned to die in the arena. We have been made a spectacle to the whole universe, to angels as well as to men* (1 Corinthians 4:9).

FOOD FOR THOUGHT: Obviously angels are watching our journey. The events of our lives are of importance because angels are interested spectators.

"Then the Lord opened Balaam's eyes,
and he saw the angel of the Lord standing in the
road with his sword drawn. So he bowed low
and fell facedown."
—*Numbers 22:31*

Chapter 19

HOW DID HE KNOW?

Harold Roberts from Fenton, Missouri, shares with us the next story of angelic help:

We were on a sightseeing tour in the nation of Israel with a group from our church here in Fenton. We were staying in a hotel in the town of Tiberias located on the Sea of Galilee.

After a wonderful Israeli dinner in our hotel dining room, my wife went back to our room, and I told her I'd be back soon and that I was going to take a walk and get some fresh air. Just outside our hotel, I met our guide who engaged me in a bit of conversation. When he asked what my plans were, he offered to give me a ride down to an ice cream parlor a bit more than four blocks away.

After I finished my treat, I decided to walk back to the hotel. I walked four blocks back in the direction of the hotel. Completing the fourth block, I looked for the hotel, but not a sign could be found. By this time it was dark and I kept on walking. Most of the sidewalks were shaded by trees except at the end of each block where there was a streetlight.

Upon reaching the seventh block with still no hotel in sight, I sensed I was lost. Being in a strange city at night, I looked around for help or at least somebody to ask for directions. There was no one—just darkness—except for the circles of light at the end of each block. I began to pray and asked the Lord for help.

As I approached the next lighted corner, block number eight by this time, I saw a figure of a man. I couldn't make out his features in the darkness, but I saw his shape. He was looking directly at me. He didn't say anything but motioned for me to follow him. Understandably, I was a bit apprehensive, but then a strange peace and calm seemed to settle over me. This seemed to indicate to me it would be all right to follow him.

He turned to the right, down a narrow dark street and motioned with his right hand for me to follow. He always made sure he kept a certain distance between us. When he came to the end of this block, he crossed the street and stood on the opposite corner under the streetlight and pointed with his hand. I looked in the direction he was pointing and sure enough, there was our hotel! I looked back in his direction to express my thanks, but he was gone! Vanished! I had looked away for not more than two or three seconds. He was simply gone.

By this time, my wife had become alarmed and wondered why I had been gone so long, so she was relieved when she saw me return. I shared with her my little adventure, right down to the details of the strange, silent man who gave me directions.

As I have looked back on this experience, I have a number of questions. How did he know I needed help?

How did he know what I was attempting to find? How did he know, without asking me, what I needed? How was it possible for him to disappear so quickly? The only logical explanation that satisfies all my questions is I believe with all my heart he was an angel—a silent, quiet angel sent on a mission of mercy.

When the angel of the Lord did not show himself again to Manoah and his wife, Manoah realized that it was the angel of the Lord (Judges 13:21).

FOOD FOR THOUGHT: There is absolutely no way to know how many times angels might have been involved in our lives. One might be right at your side, helping you turn the pages of this book. Awesome! Wouldn't it be some kind of an honor? We will never know for sure because we understand angels are spirit beings, and most of the time they are invisible. Sometimes angels can show up disguised as ordinary human beings. This is shown often in the Bible, as in the case of Manoah and his wife, parents of Samson, when the angel showed up. In fact they invited him to stay for dinner. Read the story to discover how the angel exited this scene!

"When angels visit us, we do not hear
the rustle of wings, nor feel the feathery touch
of the breast of a dove; but we know
their presence by the love
they create in
our hearts."
—*Anonymous*

Chapter 20

THE ANGEL PORTER

Here's a story from Cindy and Harold (names changed), a couple who were traveling by train to Mainhausen, Germany:

We knew we had to change trains about midway and take a train going in the opposite direction.

The train station was designed with two sets of tracks and a concrete platform, and another two sets of tracks and then another platform. To get from one platform to the other, you had to go down about twenty-five steps to a concrete corridor or tunnel that went under the tracks and up twenty-five steps to the next platform.

While we were waiting for our next train on the first platform, we discovered, by looking at the overhead monitor, that we were on the wrong platform. Our train was loading on the next platform, about ready to pull out. We had to quickly move to the next platform to catch the correct train.

Between us we had six heavy suitcases to move. Quickly I grabbed two, about all I could carry, while my wife stayed with the remaining four. I hurried down the steps and struggled up the next set of steps. I dropped the two and turned to go back to the steps to get another two. I needed three trips to carry all six across and prayed I would have enough strength to do this quickly. At the top of the steps going back down, I met a man coming rapidly, almost running and taking two steps at a time, with our four suitcases. He had one under each arm and one in each hand. He walked right by me without a word or nod and set the four down next to the two I had carried.

I looked at my wife, who had followed him, as if to ask, "Who is this?"

In reply, she simply shrugged her shoulders.

Then I turned to thank the man and he was gone! Now there were only four other people on this platform with nowhere to go, no place to hide, no door to quickly duck into. He just vanished!

My wife told me, "All of a sudden he appeared. I hadn't seen him coming. He motioned for me to follow and just picked up the four suitcases as if they had been empty. I just followed him."

I was so surprised that I didn't get a close look at him as he came up the stairs with those suitcases. It certainly didn't appear as though there was anything unusual about him. I judged him to be of average size and build. Our suitcases had been packed to the brim with goodies we were taking to friends, as well as our souvenirs. They were heavy—seventy pounds was the limit of weight for our airlines and they were just at that weight.

I calculated the combined weight of the four suitcases to be about 280 pounds, more or less. Now, I don't know very many men who could pick up 280 pounds and run up and down steps with this kind of load. I just don't understand how he could have carried them so quickly or all four at the same time.

The only solution that makes any sense to us is this must have been some kind of super being. We later concluded during the train ride that this just had to have been an angel to the rescue.

There was a violent earthquake, for an angel of the Lord came down from heaven and, going to the tomb, rolled back the stone and sat on it. His appearance was like lightning, and his clothes were white as snow. The guards were so afraid of him that they shook and became like dead men (Matthew 28:2-4).

FOOD FOR THOUGHT: Can angels do heavy lifting? The biblical account above says an angel rolled back the heavy stone that had been sealed to shut up the tomb of Jesus. So why not couldn't an angel carry four heavy suitcases? Aren't the variety of ways in which angels help out folks in need interesting?

"Then the woman went to her husband and told him, 'A man of God came to me. He looked like an angel of God, very awesome. I didn't ask him where he came from, and he didn't tell me his name.'"

—*Judges 13:6*

Chapter 21

DO ALL ANGELS
HAVE NAMES?

Evelyn from Clare, Iowa, says that she had a spiritual, visual experience with angels take place in her church. Here is her story:

One Sunday as we were worshiping and ministering to the Lord through music, I looked around, especially at the windows. I couldn't believe my eyes. Our church is colonial in design and has eight tall windows on each side of the sanctuary, and is quite beautiful.

Gradually it seemed as though the light got brighter in each window, and quickly angel warriors in white appeared to be standing in each one. They filled the windows and were standing at attention. In front of each of them were spears or other weapons.

I looked over at my husband and others, but nobody seemed to have seen what I was seeing. Later, on the way home from church, I told my husband about the angels appearing, and he hadn't seen them. I really don't know what this meant or what kind of a message it was bringing to us, but it sure inspired me.

After thinking about this, I wondered: *What were the names of those angels who made their visit that day to our church?*

Good question: Are all the angels named? We know from the Bible there are apparently ranks of angels—seraphim, cherubim, and archangels. The Bible also talks of thrones, dominions, princes, powers, and virtues. We also know that Gabriel, Michael, and Lucifer, at least, are specifically named.

But there are numbers of angels who have been named through myth, legend, history, oral histories, and more sources, as well as in the Bible. The following is but a short sample:

Abdiel: So named by John Milton in his poem *Paradise Lost*. He was supposedly second in command to Lucifer but eventually flew away to become an angel in heaven; in fact, he was the only one to abandon Lucifer.

Af: According to Jewish legend, Af is the angel of death sent on his missions by the archangel Uriel.

Apollyon: He is often called "The Destroyer" and is found in Revelation 9:11 as the "Angel of the Abyss."

Bardiel: This name is taken from a writing called the "Book of Enoch" and is considered to be the angel of lightning.

Beelzebub: Originally, he was worshiped as a Philistine god or deity. The name means "lord of the flies." In the New Testament (Matthew 12:24) Beelzebub is known as "the prince of demons."

Chamuel: He is believed to be the angel who wrestled with Jacob in the Book of Genesis and is also believed to be the angel who comforted Christ in the Garden of Gethsemane.

Gabriel: Most likely the most prominent angel in the Bible whose name means "God is our strength." He assisted Daniel; he was the angel who appeared to Mary and will appear blowing the final trumpet of judgment. Jewish legend says he parted the Red Sea for Moses and the children of Israel.

Jophiel: He is believed to be the angel who drove Adam and Eve out of the garden of Eden. He is symbolized by the flaming sword and was the guard of the tree of knowledge.

Michael: He is one of the specifically named angels in the Bible. His name is in the form of a question, "Who Is God?" He is believed to be the first and most powerful of God's created beings. He is considered to be the protector of righteousness.

Raphael: The name means "God has healed." He is not named in the Bible but is considered by many scholars to be the guardian angel of the human race. He is said to particularly love young people.

Satan: Also known as "Lucifer" or "The Devil" or "The Angel of Light." He is the very epitome of evil. He was a highly honored angel until his tragic downfall, which was caused by pride and the fact that he wanted to be God. You can read the account in Isaiah 14:12-20.

Uriel: His name means "God's Light" or "Fire of God." He is not named in the Bible, but the Jewish religion recognizes him. According to them he was the messenger sent to warn Noah of the coming flood.

Wormwood: This angel is not referred to directly, but is mentioned as a "star." Wormwood, according to the Book of Revelation, will be active in the final wrap-up of this world as we know it. This is to take place before the final coming of Jesus Christ and after the opening of the seventh seal. He appears as a flaming star that poisons the world's water supply and causes much death and destruction in these final days.

Do all angels have names? I don't know, but if you were to name them, I'm sure the listing would fill volumes. Jesus mentioned at one time that He could call on "legions" of angels for help. So how many angels are there in heaven? These and other such questions caused many theological discussions in the past. And there was much controversy surrounding such speculations. Some even argued over how many angels could dance on the head of a pin.

Once more, the bottom line is that curiosity is great but don't let it lead you astray from the solid teachings of the Bible, God's final Word on angels and their ministries and their names. I remind you that angels are not to be worshiped, great as they are—only God is worthy of worship!

"An angel is an intelligent essence, always
in motion. It has free will, is incorporeal, serves God,
and has been bestowed with immortality.
Only the Creator understands
its true nature."
—*John of Damascus*

Chapter 22

MYSTERIOUS GRANDSONS

This is another angel story that has taken on a life of its own like an urban legend. I have heard a number of versions in a number of different settings and locations, but all contain the same elements. So, let's share the story set in Chicago. What makes this story different is the proof is supposedly still evident to this day, if you know where to look. Don't miss the ending! The story goes like this:

The story took place in the 1870s. It supposedly involved a priest, Arnold Damien, and the Society of Jesus. He is the priest who purportedly founded an "altar boy" society. He taught many young boys the tradition of the Mass and how they were to assist the priest with their duties.

Years of faithful service passed and finally Father Damien went into retirement. He ministered only on special occasions and served as a mentor to young priests.

One dark, stormy night, the doorbell rang at the rectory and the young assistant answered the door to find two young boys on the steps. They explained their grandmother was really sick, and she was in need of a priest because she would not last through the night.

The assistant said, "It's too cold and rainy tonight, boys. I'll make sure to send a priest tomorrow."

But behind the assistant stood the retired old priest listening to the conversation. Father Damien went to the door and told the boys, "I'll come right now. Come in to warm yourself while I get ready."

Not long afterwards, the two boys led the priest through the deserted wet streets until they came to an old apartment house about a mile from the rectory. The boys pointed to a window on the top story of the old building and told him he would find their grandmother there.

The priest went into the building, but the boys didn't follow. He climbed the narrow winding staircase and found the door open. He gently knocked and entered to find an elderly woman. She was cold, very sick, and seemed close to death. He ministered to her and gave her communion.

"Father," she managed to whisper, "how did you happen to come here? Some people in the building know I'm sick, but none of them are Catholic."

He stared at her strangely, then said, "Your two grandsons came for me and I followed them here. They told me you could be found in this apartment."

She closed her eyes and with a smile said, "Father, I had two grandsons who were altar boys at Holy Family Church, but they both died years ago."

Here's the clincher! I've been told the Holy Family Church still stands just west of the University of Illinois'

Circle Campus on Roosevelt Road. And further, I've been told that if you visit the sanctuary, high over the entrance you will see the statues of two altar boys, one on each side, holding candles while they face each other. Supposedly these statues were commissioned by Father Damien in honor of what he had considered to have been the visit of two angels disguised as altar boys one cold, dark, rainy night in Chicago in the 1870s.

> *Suddenly an angel of the Lord appeared and a light shone in the cell. He struck Peter on the side and woke him up. "Quick, get up!" he said, and the chains fell off Peter's wrists. Then the angel said to him, "Put on your clothes and sandals." And Peter did so. "Wrap your cloak around you and follow me," the angel told him. Peter followed him out of the prison, but he had no idea that what the angel was doing was really happening" (Acts 12:7-9).*

FOOD FOR THOUGHT: Did some architect originally plan the statues of the altar boys and the story has been told to fit the statues? Or is it the other way around, as in the story? Whatever, it's a great story. And in the Bible, many of the angel occurrences involve an action, such as with the angel who commanded Peter to get dressed and follow him.

"Sometimes, a man's understanding is
enlightened by an angel to know what is good,
but it is not instructed as to the reason why.
But sometimes he is instructed by angelic
illumination, both that this act is good
and as to the reason why it is good."
— *St. Thomas Aquinas*

Chapter 23

TWO AFRICAN ANGELS

The place is the Sudan, in Northeast Africa; the city is Khartoum; the time is 1989 during the winter season. It's the country where an indigenous missionary family was born—father, mother, and four children. Let's hear their story as this Sudanese woman, now living as a naturalized citizen in the United States, tells it:

Our home had been used as a place of rest and refuge for a number of missionaries, in particular the Sudan Interior Mission. The situation was critical because of the ruling Muslim government that demanded our presence in the mission to divert attention from the foreign missionaries.

It so happens the mention of angels is a popular topic among us. Everybody—both Muslims and Christians—believed in angels. It was a subject which could likely be discussed almost every day.

It was also at this critical time that the door had opened for us to migrate to the United States. Much was happening, events were swirling about us over which we didn't seem to have much control, and it was nearing the time when three of our children were to leave. It was at this time the government decided to take away from us our adopted four-year-old son, Samir, and place him in a Muslim family for their adoption. In so doing he was to be raised as a Muslim, not a Christian.

On top of this, one of our children was sick and confined to a bedroom on the ground floor. I had worries upon worries. Panic and fear began to grip my heart.

One evening this cup of suffering and weariness just overflowed. I went into my closet in our bedroom to pray. I prayed until I fell asleep.

I was awakened suddenly! I saw a light coming in from the doors to the closed balcony. Two figures stood against the drawn curtains. My heart was beating with the thought that this was a night robbery. I sat up and covered my face with my hands and then slowly opened them. The two figures came nearer. They were tall, and their heads were wrapped in traditional African floral turbans matching their long elaborate robes. They spoke in a quiet tone in our native language.

One of them said, "Do not be afraid."

The other said, "We are sent to encourage you. God wants you to know this: YOU ARE NOT ALONE!"

I was trembling and asked, "Are you angels? If you are, then come and stand behind the big chair."

To my shock and amazement, they glided and danced their way to the chair. They were beautiful and silhouetted against the light they brought with them. Then and there I sensed a great peace of God. I asked, "Why are you dressed so?"

The second angel replied, "This is how we were sent here," obviously referring to Africa, where floral designs are very traditional.

The other angel spoke, "You are loved, both you and your family. We encourage your faith because you encourage the helpless and insecure."

Then they disappeared, gradually out of my sight as silently as they had entered. I was alone once more, but I was completely refreshed in body and in spirit. I was thankful that now I could face the remainder of what was before us.

On the twenty-fourth day of the first month, as I was standing on the bank of the great river, the Tigris, I looked up and there before me was a man dressed in linen, with a belt of the finest gold around his waist. He body was like chrysolite, his face like lightning, his eyes like flaming torches, his arms and legs like the gleam of burnished bronze, and his voice like the sound of a multitude. I, Daniel, was the only one who saw the vision; the men with me did not see it, but such terror overwhelmed them that they fled and hid themselves (Daniel 10:4-7).

FOOD FOR THOUGHT: Daniel was the only one who saw the angel, but others felt the effect of that presence. Most angel stories have to do with a single person who may have been the only one to experience the appearance. Once again, we must trust the messenger as to what they have seen or experienced. We have attempted to weed out any stories that didn't pass the biblical test.

"We shall find peace. We shall hear the angels, we shall see the sky sparkling with diamonds."
—*Anton Pavlovich Chekhov*

Chapter 24

SNATCHED FROM
THE OCEAN OF FIRE

In 1924, while working near a logging camp in Oregon, Tom Williams fell thirty-five feet from a railroad trestle, head first, and struck a steel pipe. He then bounced and fell another twenty feet into a twelve-foot-deep tank of water.

He lay on the bottom of the tank with a crushed skull and a rib-punctured lung for more than an hour. He was pulled out and taken to the nearest hospital where doctors found no water in his lungs. Evidently he had been dead when he entered the water or knocked unconscious.

A nearby Christian friend was notified of his death. She quickly ran to the hospital, knelt by his side, and prayed that God would raise him from the dead. In fact, in her prayer, she boldly told God she refused to let Tom die in his spiritual condition because he was not a Christian. She even told God she had already spent too many hours in prayer for Him to let Tom die like this.

Tom had already been covered over with a sheet, and his body was ready to be taken to the morgue. The attending doctor was about to ask some security people to drag this praying lady away from the scene. He thought she might have been in shock or her mind had snapped. Suddenly Tom began to speak and removed the sheet from his face!

The lady began to praise God rather loudly, and the doctor suddenly needed his own doctor! He knew there had to be a God when he saw the dead man return to life, and so the doctor accepted Christ as his Savior.

Tom eventually related what happened. The last thing he remembered was falling from the trestle. When he came to he was standing on a cliff overlooking an ocean of fire. As far as he could see in any direction there were rolling billows of blue, orange, and yellow flames of fire. Out of the fire he saw his uncle and a pal approach him. The uncle had been dead seven years and the friend for three years. The flames were about halfway between their ankles and knees.

Tom instantly knew he was in hell, and a feeling of despair came over him. He communicated with his uncle and friend by thought transfer rather than by words.

Then Tom looked up and saw Jesus Christ crossing this ocean of fire. He thought, *If only I can get Jesus to look at me, He will get me out of here.* Jesus was almost across the abyss, and Tom felt the dread of eternal doom sweep over him.

But just before Jesus disappeared, He turned and looked at Tom! Instantly Tom was propelled out of the ocean of fire. His spirit entered his body, sort of like walking through a door. It was at this moment he heard his friend praying for him and he removed the sheet from over his head and spoke to her. Within five days Tom walked out of the hospital completely healed with no aftereffects.

Because of this miraculous experience in his life, Tom became a Christian and trained to become a minister. He spent the rest of his life sharing this story and ministering to people.

Then death and Hades were thrown into the lake of fire. The lake of fire is the second death. If anyone's name was not found written in the book of life, he was thrown into the lake of fire (Revelation 20:14-15).

FOOD FOR THOUGHT: Is your name written in the book of life? If not, why not? You don't know how to have your name written there? It's simple—if you confess with your mouth, "Jesus is Lord," and believe in your heart that God raised Him from the dead, you will be saved! It's with your heart that you believe and are justified, and it is with your mouth that you confess and are saved. And we have this positive assurance—everyone who calls on the name of the Lord will be saved (see Romans 10:9-10, 13).

"Do not forget to entertain
strangers, for by so doing
some people have entertained
angels without knowing it."
—*Hebrews 13:2*

Chapter 25

HAVE YOU ENTERTAINED ANGELS?

Gene and Judy lived in a southern state and were the parents of six kids ranging in age from five to fifteen. They were a churchgoing, church-loving family. Gene had worked at the local lumber mill for a number of years, and when it folded, he was left with nothing but odd jobs to make a living.

One day he had a small job in town repairing a car. On this day Judy was doing the laundry and had invited some church ladies over for an afternoon coffee. Their conversation was broken when Judy's oldest came running into the house, "Mom," she said, "there's a man coming around to the back door. Says he's got to talk to you."

Immediately these well-meaning church ladies warned, "Be careful. Don't have anythin' to do with a man who's comin' beggin'! Now hear!"

At the back door stood an elderly African-American man with graying hair and soft, warm eyes. "Ma'am, sorry to bother you, but my truck broke down, and I'm walking to town. I would appreciate it if you could give me some water and a bit of food if you could spare it."

Judy was stunned. She found herself hesitant to do the right thing because she had been influenced by the ladies. Instead of getting the water and food, she stood there. Their eyes met and the old man waited a few seconds and then silently turned away. Judy felt ashamed as she went back to the table, but even worse was the condemning look she received from her oldest daughter.

Quickly she grabbed a pitcher of lemonade and some cookies and ran out the front door to find the old man on his knees with the rest of the children around him listening as he told them a Bible story. She offered the cookies and lemonade and told the man to wait as she went back in the house to prepare a sack lunch for him. She returned and said, "I'm sorry about the way I acted."

"That's all right," he said. "Too many people are influenced by others. But unlike some, you have overcome it, and this speaks well for you."

That night Gene had wonderful news! The car he had repaired belonged to a man whose brother ran a repair shop and happened to be looking for a good mechanic. He hired Gene on the spot!

Later, Judy told Gene about the events of the afternoon. When she was finished, he asked, "Did you say this was an elderly black man? Kind-looking eyes and gray hair?" He jumped out of bed and went through his pockets until he found a piece of folded paper that he handed to Judy.

He said, "I met that man walking down the road when I came from town. He waved me over and gave this to me. I took the note and quickly read it. When I looked up, he was gone! Just disappeared! I got out of the car and looked up and down the road. I could see for a good mile or more in each direction, but he was gone! I thought it strange but haven't had time to think any more about it."

Judy unfolded the note and began to cry as she read it. Here's what it said: "Do not forget to entertain strangers, for by so doing some people have entertained angels without knowing it."

Keep on loving each other as brothers. Do not forget to entertain strangers, for by so doing some people have entertained angels without knowing it. Remember those in prison as if you were their fellow prisoners, and those who are mistreated as if you yourselves were suffering (Hebrews 13:1-3).

FOOD FOR THOUGHT: How many strangers have you entertained that in reality were angels? In today's world we are always cautioned about strangers and told to avoid them. But does that make it right? We need to be careful, yes. But if and when you do open your heart to strangers, you might be having a wonderful adventure. Who knows?

"Our valleys may be filled with foes and tears;
but we can lift our eyes to the hills to see God
and the angels, heaven's spectators,
who support us according to God's
infinite wisdom as they prepare
our welcome home."
—*Billy Graham*

Chapter 26

ANGELS COMING FOR TO TAKE ME HOME

The above words are taken from a wonderful, old spiritual. But there may be more truth than wishful thinking in it in regard to the home-going of some of God's wonderful people. Let's take a quick look at some bedside or even deathbed experiences.

When D. L. Moody, the evangelist, was aware death was nearing he said, "Earth recedes, heaven opens before me." To those who had gathered at his bedside, it seemed as if he were dreaming, but he said, "No, this is no dream. It is beautiful; it is like a trance. If this is death, it is sweet. There is no valley here. God is calling me, and I must go."

After having been given up for dead, Moody revived long enough to indicate that God permitted him to see beyond this life. He said he had been "within the gates and beyond the portals and caught a glimpse of familiar faces whom he had loved and in the presence of a great heavenly host."

Phillips Brooks, the composer of "O Little Town of Bethlehem," was a great preacher/orator of the nineteenth century. When he died, a little girl of five told her mother, "Mother, how happy the angels will be!"

Billy Graham wrote "When my maternal grandmother died, the room seemed to fill with a heavenly light. She sat up in bed and almost laughingly said, 'I see Jesus. He has His arms outstretched toward me. I see Ben (her husband who had died some years earlier) and I see angels.' She slumped over, absent from the body but present with the Lord."

Lucille O'Neil, had a beautiful experience at death. She had been in a tubercular hospital for some years. The night before her death she talked about the sweet-smelling fragrance of the beautiful flowers and the angel who stood at the pathway leading through the flower garden. Occasionally, the angel waved to her. "It was as if they were in the room with me," she said. Later she pointed to the ceiling and said, "There the angel is now, waving again. He is standing among the most beautiful roses I have ever seen. Can you smell the roses?"

Sibil Spruill from Houston was taken to Herman Hospital for treatment following a severe asthma attack. She explained her experience at death as "something so beautiful and pleasant that there are not sufficient descriptive terms in man's language to aptly relate the reality of heaven." She saw white robes on manlike forms but saw no faces. After being ushered into an atmosphere of brightness and beauty, she eventually came to a resting place that seemed to be a waiting area before entering heaven. The white-robed angels stood on either side of her as she looked upon the breathtaking beauty of the heavenly scene before her.

The angels on either side of her seemed to be discussing whether to take her into the beautiful brightness that stretched before her or to return her to earth. The same robed angelic forms then lifted her from the place where she was standing and moved swiftly toward earth. An instant later she found her spirit entering her body again, in the same way it had departed, almost as if a vacuum had pulled it into the body.

When she awoke, the asthma attack was gone! And later, she discovered she had been completely healed of asthma and lived for many more years!

> *Therefore we are always confident and know that as long as we are at home in the body we are away from the Lord. We live by faith, not by sight. We are confident, I say, and would prefer to be away from the body and at home with the Lord. So we make it our goal to please Him, whether we are at home in the body or away from it. For we must all appear before the judgment seat of Christ, that each one may receive what is due him for the things done while in the body, whether good or bad* (2 Corinthians 5:6-10).

FOOD FOR THOUGHT: I believe that death can be a beautiful experience! With that belief we can look forward to it and welcome it with anticipation. The Bible plainly states, "Precious in the sight of the Lord is the death of His saints" (Psalm 116:15). David said it so well for all of us, "Even though I walk through the valley of the shadow of death, I will fear no evil, for You are with me" (Psalm 23:4). Are you ready for life or death? No one is really ready to die who has not placed confidence in the sacrifice of Jesus Christ for their sins. Death is our greatest crisis. And we have the assurance that He will have His angels ready to gather us in their arms and carry us gloriously into our heavenly reward! Anticipate it! It's awesome to contemplate!